My Holy Land Bucket List

This Adventure Journal Belongs To:

_____

"O God, You are more awesome than Your holy places. The God of Israel is He who gives strength and power to His people. Blessed be God!"

Psalm 68:35 NKJV

Plan Your Holy Land Adventure!

The Holy Land is the geographic heartland of faith for millions of visitors each year. Traveling to this Biblical land and being able to walk in the actual footsteps of Jesus is on the Bucket List for many Christians. This book is designed to help make this faith filled journey unique and special to each individual. Whether you want to visit Bethlehem, Old City Jerusalem, Via Dolorosa, experience a traditional Shabbat, float in the Dead Sea, or enjoy Tel-Aviv's incredible food scene – this 'Holy Land Bucket List' can be used as a tool to outline, plan and detail each memory of your journey.

Inside this 'Holy Land Bucket List' you will find:

- Over 170 suggested destination points and unique adventures for your itinerary inspiration
- 100 pages dedicated for you to record up to 50 Holy Land Bucket List experiences
- Additional bulleted pages to create your own Bucket List ideas
- More pages for detailing unique highlights and memories of your trip

Dream no longer! Plan your Holy Land adventure and be transported back to the days of Biblical history!

Shalom!

Israel and Neighboring Regions

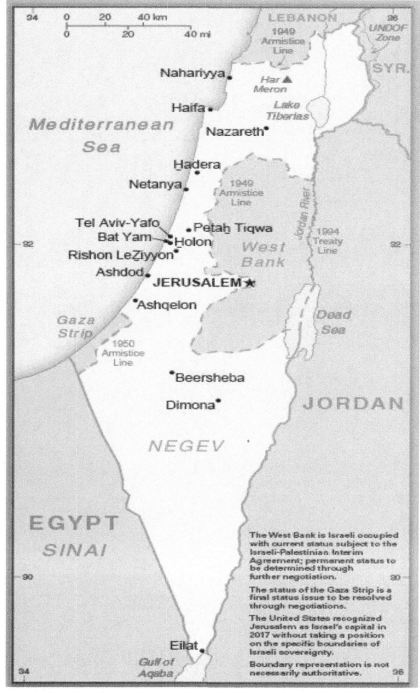

The World Factbook 2020. Washington, DC: Central Intelligence Agency, 2020.
https://www.cia.gov/library/publications/resources/the-world-factbook/index.html

Holy Land Points of Interest

Northern Israel Region

- ❏ **Acre's Old City (Akko)**- Set among seaside cliffs, this old city is also home to the Templars Underground Tunnel.
- ❏ **Atlit Yam** - Coastal town South of Haifa where you can dive to see the submerged ruins of a Neolithic coastal settlement.
- ❏ **Banias Nature Reserve** – See the Banias Waterfall and ruins of ancient cities located near Mt. Hermon.
- ❏ **Beit She'an National Park & Archeological Site** - This Archeological Site was where the ancient town of Scitopolis was excavated and also boasts a 2nd century Roman theater. In the Biblical account of King Saul, he and his three sons were hung on the walls of Beit She'an.
- ❏ **Bethsaida** - This ancient fishing village on the Sea of Galilee is known as the birthplace of three of the Apostles: Peter, Andrew and Philip.
- ❏ **Caesarea Philippi** - 30 miles North of the Sea of Galilee where Jesus revealed to His disciples that He was the Jewish Messiah.
- ❏ **Cana (Kafr Kanna)** - Associated with the New Testament village of Cana where Jesus turned water into wine at the marriage feast.
- ❏ **Capernaum** - Where Jesus recruited his first disciples from fishermen and where Jesus healed Peter's mother-in-law.

Holy Land Points of Interest

Northern Israel Region

- ❏ **Cave of Elijah** - The cave where Elijah took refuge while in the wilderness after travelling 40 days and nights as told in the Biblical account of 1 Kings 19:8.
- ❏ **Gamla National Park** - This ancient Jewish city was believed to be a fort during the Syrian wars. The nature reserve and archaeological site is home to raptors and vultures.
- ❏ **Golan Heights** -Enjoy vistas of beautiful canyons and greenery near the Syrian border.
- ❏ **Haifa** - Israel's third largest city set on the slopes of Mount Carmel with views of the Mediterranean Sea. Some call it 'Israel's San Francisco'.
- ❏ **Haifa - Baha'i Gardens** -Beautiful gardens featuring 19 terraces of geometric flower beds leading to the domed Bahai shrine on Mount Carmel.
- ❏ **Jezreel Valley and Megiddo** - A fertile valley known for immense beauty and historic importance. Named in the Bible as the valley where Gideon lived and where many battles took place - also noted in the Bible as the valley where the final battle of Armageddon will take place.
- ❏ **Magdala (Migdal)** - An ancient settlement on the coast of the Sea of Galilee. Rich in history for both Jews and Christians, it is believed to be the birthplace of Mary Magdalene.

Holy Land Points of Interest

Northern Israel Region

- ❑ **Mount Arbel National Park -** Majestic views of the Galilee region - historical site on the slope of Mount Arbel where Jews hid in caves when they fought against the Greeks and Romans and also the site of an ancient synogogue.
- ❑ **Mount Bental** - A popular mountain peak with panoramic views of the Golan Heights, Mount Hermon and upper Galilee.
- ❑ **Mount of Beatitudes** - The location where Jesus gave the Sermon on the Mount and declared the Beatitudes as told in the Gospel of Matthew.
- ❑ **Mount Carmel** - Referenced in the Bible as the site where the prophet Elijah prays for God to send fire to consume his water drenched offering in a confrontation with 850 of King Ahab's pagan prophets.
- ❑ **Mount Gilboa** - Where King Saul and his son died by their own hands during a battle with the Philistines.
- ❑ **Mount Precipice** - Spectacular view of Nazareth - also believed to have been the place where the mob tried to throw Jesus of this peak.
- ❑ **Mount Tabor** - The site of the battle between the Israelite army and the Canaanites. Also believed to be the site of the transfiguration of Jesus.

Holy Land Points of Interest

Northern Israel Region

- ❑ **Mount Hermon** - The highest mountain of Israel with a ski resort located between Syria & Lebanon surrounded by the Hermon nature reserve.
- ❑ **Nazareth** - A city steeped in Biblical history where the angel Gabriel told Mary that she would give birth to Jesus.
- ❑ **Nazareth - Mary's Well** - This village well is believed by some to have been visited daily by Mary, many times accompanied by her son Jesus.
- ❑ **Nazareth - St. Joseph's Church** - Believed to be the site where Joseph had his carpentry workshop.
- ❑ **Nazareth - Synagogue Church** - Supposed to be the site where Jesus studied and prayed.
- ❑ **Nazareth - Basilica of the Anunciation** - Some believe this is where the Angel Gabriel announced to Mary that she would give birth to the Messiah, Jesus.
- ❑ **Nazareth Village** - This open-air museum reconstructs daily life in the time of Jesus.
- ❑ **Nimrod Fortress** – Medieval castle located on the southern slopes of Mount Hermon overlooking the Golan Heights.
- ❑ **Safed** - Known as the Capital of the Galilee, this city has a rich 2000 year old history. Explore the old city with cobblestone streets, ancient synagogues and many art galleries.

Holy Land Points of Interest

Northern Israel Region

- ❏ **Sea of Galilee** - Where Jesus walked on water, calmed the storm and fed the multitudes. See an ancient fishing boat believed to be from the time of Christ and take a boat tour of the Sea of Galilee.
- ❏ **Stella Maris Monastery** - A Carmelite monastery with a muraled dome roof and ornate stained glass. Under the altar is the cave where Prophet Elijah lived during the time of the famous confrontation with the priests of Baal.
- ❏ **Tabgha** - Where Jesus multiplied the loaves and fish. Also where Jesus asked Peter to 'Feed My Sheep'.
- ❏ **Tiberias** - Rich in both Jewish and Christian history, it is known as one of Judaism's four holiest cities.
- ❏ **Tiberias - Hamat Tiberias National Park** - An ancient archaeological site known for natural hot springs and an ancient synagogue dating back to when Tiberias was the seat of the Sanhedrin.
- ❏ **Tyre and Sidon** - Tyre had ancient fame for its rare purple dye. These coastal cities have a prophetic Biblical history.
- ❏ **Zippori National Park** - Site of historical architecture - known as 'the ornament of all Galilee'. Featuring beautiful mosaics throughout the architecture including a Biblical mosaic in an ancient synagogue.

Holy Land Points of Interest

Northern Israel Region

❑ _____

❑ _____

❑ _____

❑ _____

❑ _____

❑ _____

❑ _____

❑ _____

❑ _____

❑ _____

❑ _____

❑ _____

❑ _____

❑ _____

Holy Land Points of Interest
Northern Israel Region: Mediterranean

- ☐ **Caesarea Aqueduct** - This historic raised aqueduct brought running water to the old city of Caesarea.
- ☐ **Caesarea Harbor National Park** - King Herod built this great city and harbor during his reign – this coastal park offers great views of the Mediterranean.
- ☐ **Caesarea Maritima Museum** - Home to the largest collection of archeological artifacts.
- ☐ **Caesarea National Park** - A magnificent port city that was built by Herod the Great which is also home to the Roman Amphitheater.
- ☐ **Caesarea Ralli Museums** – Renowned art museum featuring the works of Dali, Rodin, Arman and Masson.
- ☐ **Old City Gallery Caesarea** - Features Israeli authentic artists.
- ☐ _____
- ☐ _____
- ☐ _____
- ☐ _____
- ☐ _____
- ☐ _____

Holy Land Points of Interest

Central Israel Region: Mediterranean

- ❏ **Ashkelon** - South of Tel Aviv, this coastal town is the oldest and largest seaport in Canaan.
- ❏ **Beit Hatfutsot (The Diaspora Museum)** - This beautiful museum traces the history and origins of the Jewish people.
- ❏ **Carmel Market** - Tel Aviv's largest open-air marketplace. Great place to buy your spices!
- ❏ **Eretz Israel Museum** - In addition to historical artifacts and a planetarium, this museum is also an active archaeological facility.
- ❏ **Jaffa's Old City and Old Port** - Named after Noah's son who built the city after the Flood - it is also here that Jonah had his adventure with the whale.
- ❏ **Nahalat Binyamin Market** - This historic market is the largest arts and crafts market in Israel.
- ❏ **Neve Tzedek** - Boutique shops, cafes and art galleries in this beautiful neighborhood - described as Tel Aviv's SoHo.
- ❏ **Old Tel Aviv Port** - Originally Tel Aviv's main port to the Mediterranean - the area is now known as a revitalized entertainment district with shops, cafes and restaurants.
- ❏ **Palmach Museum** - Visit here to learn more about Israel's military history and how the region was protected from Nazi invasion.
- ❏ **Rabin Square** - A memorial marking where the former Prime Minister Yitzhak Rabin was assassinated.

Holy Land Points of Interest

Central Israel Region: Mediterranean

- ☐ **Tel Aviv** - One of the biggest cities in Israel - About 40 minutes outside of Jerusalem.
- ☐ **Tel Aviv Beaches** - over 16 stunning beaches ready for a day of relaxation.
- ☐ **Tel Aviv Museum of Art** - Both Local and international artists from the 16th century to the present.
- ☐ **The Tayelet** - 3-mile long beach boardwalk with spectacular views of the Mediterranean.
- ☐ **White City** - An architectural wonder with a collection of International Style houses.
- ☐ **Yitzhak Rabin Center** - This museum details the life of the late Israeli Prime Minister Yitzhak Rabin with programs that inspire civil exchange about the complex Israeli society.
- ☐ _____
- ☐ _____
- ☐ _____
- ☐ _____
- ☐ _____
- ☐ _____
- ☐ _____

Holy Land Points of Interest

Central Israel Region: Jerusalem

- [ ] **Biblical Museum of Natural History** - Exhibits that are described as part zoo, part natural history and part Torah education. Featuring animals of the Scriptures. In Beit Shemesh, about 30 minutes from Jersualem.
- [ ] **Ein Karem** - The hometown village of John the Baptist and site of the Church of St. John the Baptist, Church of the Visitation and Mary's Spring.
- [ ] **Israel Museum** - Home to parts of the Dead Sea Scrolls and a display of a model of the second temple.
- [ ] **Kidron Valley** - Rich in Old Testament Biblical history, this valley features ancient tombs, monuments and olive groves leading up to the Mount of Olives.
- [ ] **Russian Compound** - Outside the walls of the Old City, also includes a Russian consulate and an Orthodox cathedral.
- [ ] **Stalactite Cave Nature Reserve (Avshalom Cave/Soreq Cave)** - Take a guided tour through a limestone cave featuring stalactites and stalagmites. About 35 minutes from Jerusalem.
- [ ] **The Knesset - Israel's Parliament** - Offers free themed tours and activities in multiple languages so visitors can learn more about Israeli democracy.

Holy Land Points of Interest

Central Israel Region: Jerusalem

❑ **The Rekevet Trail (Rail Trail)** - Former railroad racks changed into running trails, bike paths and pedestrian paths.

❑ **Yad Vashem** - Holocaust museum and memorial with guided tours and historical exhibits.

❑ _____

❑ _____

❑ _____

❑ _____

❑ _____

❑ _____

❑ _____

❑ _____

❑ _____

❑ _____

❑ _____

❑ _____

Holy Land Points of Interest

Central Israel Region: Jerusalem Old City

- [ ] **Chapel of the Ascension** - A historic dome shrine where Jesus ascended at the top of Mount Olives overlooking the Old City.
- [ ] **Church of All Nations (Basilica of the Agony)** – Just outside the Old City on the Mount of Olives near the Garden of Gethsemane - believed to hold the section of bedrock where Jesus prayed before his arrest.
- [ ] **Church of St. Peter in Gallicantu** - Located outside the Old City on the hillside of Mount Zion - where Peter denied Christ three times.
- [ ] **Church of the Holy Sepulchre (Calvary/Golgotha)** - Said to have been built on the site where Jesus was crucified and holds the 'Tomb of Jesus' or 'Edicule'. It houses the last stop of the Via Dolorosa pilgrimage.
- [ ] **Damascus Gate** - One of the main entrances to the Old City of Jerusalem.
- [ ] **Dome of the Rock** - A Muslim shrine built on top of the 'Foundation Stone' of the Jewish Temple. A holy site for Jews, Christians and Muslims.
- [ ] **Garden of Gethsemane** - Where Jesus prayed the night before his arrest - Located on the Mount of Olives overlooking Old Jerusalem.
- [ ] **Golden Gate** - One of the four main gated entrances into the Old City that has some controversy as it is claimed by Muslims and Jews.

Holy Land Points of Interest

Central Israel Region: Jerusalem Old City

- ❑ **House of Caiaphas** - A little known archeological site on Mount Zion just outside the walls of Old Jerusalem - Where Jesus was kept the night after his arrest. Also the location where Peter denied Jesus 3 times.
- ❑ **Jaffa Gate** - The main passageway for the Christian Quarter - a great place to enjoy a beautiful view of the Mediterranean Sea.
- ❑ **Lion's Gate (St. Stephen's Gate)** - The Eastern entry to Old Jerusalem.
- ❑ **Mount of Olives** - On a hill just across the valley from the old city. Where Jesus would gather with his disciples to pray and later where Jesus ascended to heaven after His crucifixion and resurrection.
- ❑ **Mount Zion** - Located just outside of 'Zion Gate' of Old Jerusalem - Where you can visit the Upper Room (Cenacle) where Christ celebrated the Last Supper. Also the place of King David's Tomb.
- ❑ **Pool of Bethesda** - The scene where Jesus healed a the paralyzed man who had waited for 38 years for someone to help him into the healing waters of the pool.
- ❑ **Pool of Siloam** - Where Jesus healed a man who had been blind since birth.
- ❑ **Ramparts Walks** - Explore this unique view of the city of Jerusalem from the top of the Old City walls.

Holy Land Points of Interest
Central Israel Region: Jerusalem Old City

- ☐ **Solomon's Quarries (Zedekiah's Grotto)** - A cave system under the Old City. Tradition says the stone for the first temple was quarried from here. Zedekiah, the last king of Judah, hid here from the Babylonian forces in 587 BC.
- ☐ **Temple Mount (Haram Al-Sharif)** - Sacred to the Jewish faith, this compound, built by Herod the Great, is located on what is believed to be the original site of the Jewish temple.
- ☐ **The Garden Tomb** - A rock-cut tomb unearthed in 1867 - considered by some to be the site of the burial and resurrection of Jesus. Groups can reserve a place to receive Holy Communion together.
- ☐ **Tomb of King David** - On Mount Zion just outside the Old City.
- ☐ **Tower of David (Jerusalem Citadel)** - A Citadel museum with archeological ruins dating back 2700 years. Exhibit rooms depict over 4,000 years of Jerusalem's history.
- ☐ **Via Dolorosa - Way of the Cross city walk** - Follow the path Jesus walked on the way to His crucifixion by visiting each of the nine 'Stations of the Cross'.
- ☐ **Western Wailing Wall** - A 2,000 year old retaining wall built on the western side of the Temple Mount. It is a Jewish holy site for prayer because of its proximity to where the Holy of Holies was located in the temple.

Holy Land Points of Interest

Central Israel Region: Jerusalem Old City

❑ **Zion Gate** - The main entry into the Jewish Quarter and also known as the 'Gate of King David'.

❑ _____

❑ _____

❑ _____

❑ _____

❑ _____

❑ _____

❑ _____

❑ _____

❑ _____

❑ _____

❑ _____

❑ _____

❑ _____

Holy Land Points of Interest

Central Israel Region: Bethlehem/West Bank

- ❑ **Bethlehem** - 25 minutes South of Jerusalem. Known as the 'City of David' - An archaeological site that reveals the origins of Jerusalem and the birthplace of Jesus.
- ❑ **Blessings Gift Shop and The Olive Wood Factory** - This family owned business was established in 1925 and offers beautiful gift items crafted from olive wood native to the Holy Land.
- ❑ **Jacob's Well** - The location mentioned in the New Testament where Jesus met the Samaritan woman. The well still stands today.
- ❑ **Hebron** - The site of the oldest Jewish community dating back to Biblical times. It was the first place Abraham lived after arriving in Canaan and where King David was anointed. Is also the location of the 'Tomb of the Patriarchs' where Abraham, Isaac and Jacob are buried.
- ❑ **Herodion National Park** - Herod's fortress or palace in the Judean Desert with historic archaeological finds.
- ❑ **Jericho** - A Palestinian city in the Jordan Valley named in the Old Testament Biblical account as the first town attacked by Joshua and the Israelites after they crossed the Jordan River. Also mentioned in the New Testament as the place where Jesus met the tax collector Zacchaeus.

Holy Land Points of Interest
Central Israel Region: Bethlehem/West Bank

- ❑ **Jordan River at Al-Maghtas, Jordan** - Visit the baptismal site believed to be where Jesus was baptized - also known as 'Bethany Beyond the Jordan'.
- ❑ **Mar Saba Monastery** - An historic old Greek Orthodox monastery magnificently built between the vertical rock walls of the Kidron Gorge.
- ❑ **Milk Grotto** - said to be the site where Mary, Joseph and Jesus hid before their flight into Egypt.
- ❑ **Monastery of St. George** - A 5th century monastery built on the side of a cliff in the Wadi Qelt narrow gorge.
- ❑ **Nablus** - One of Palestine's largest cities famous for traditional olive oil soap, textiles, sweets and markets.
- ❑ **Old Bethlehem Museum** - An eclectic and charming museum with exhibits of an earlier Bethlehem.
- ❑ **Shepherd's Field Church** - A church that marks the place where angels announced the birth of Jesus to the shepherds.
- ❑ **Solomon's Pools** - Pools build in ancient times to be the water supply for Jerusalem - Dated to the reign of King Solomon.
- ❑ **The Church of the Nativity** - See the birthplace of Jesus.

Holy Land Points of Interest

Central Israel Region: Bethlehem/West Bank

- ❑ **The Mount of Temptation** - Take a cable car ride to the top of this mountain believed to be the mountain in the desert where Jesus was tempted for 40 days and nights.
- ❑ **The Museum of the Good Samaritan** - Home to archeological artifacts and Byzantine mosaics. Dedicated to the history and customs of the Samaritan community.
- ❑ _____
- ❑ _____
- ❑ _____
- ❑ _____
- ❑ _____
- ❑ _____
- ❑ _____
- ❑ _____
- ❑ _____
- ❑ _____

Holy Land Points of Interest

Central Israel Region: Dead Sea

- ☐ **Dead Sea** - Relax and float your care's away in the Dead Sea while you enjoy nature's perfect spa - experience the benefits of the natural Dead Sea mud.
- ☐ **Ein Gedi Nature Reserve** - One of the most popular hiking places in Israel featuring waterfalls, botanical gardens, birds of prey and other wildlife.
- ☐ **Masada National Park** - An ancient fortress overlooking the Dead Sea. Includes the Masada Museum and King Herod's Palace.
- ☐ **Qumran National Park** - See the caves where the Bedouin boy found the Dead Sea Scrolls of the Old Testament.

☐ _____

☐ _____

☐ _____

☐ _____

☐ _____

☐ _____

☐ _____

☐ _____

Holy Land Points of Interest

Southern Israel Region

- **Beersheba (Be'er Sheva)** - This is the largest city of the Negev desert. Mentioned in the Bible as the site where Abraham made a covenant with the Philistine King Abimelech.
- **Eilat** - This resort town is at the head of the Red Sea peninsula. It boasts great coral reefs for scuba diving, dolphins and a bird festival. 20 miles North of Eilat you can hike the beautiful Red Canyon.
- **The Negev** - Take a camel ride, horseback ride or Jeep safari to the Ramon Crater. Visit the Mitzpe Ramon Visitor Center to learn about the fascinating geology that created the Ramon Crater.
- **Timna Park** - See the world's first copper mine actively mined for thousands of years - Visitors can also view tons of rock formations including Solomon's Pillars and see a life size replica of the Biblical Tabernacle accurate to the description in the Bible.
- _____

- _____

- _____

- _____

- _____

Holy Land Points of Interest

Jordan

- ❏ **Ajloun Castle** - 12th Century Muslim Castle in Northern Jordan.
- ❏ **Amman** - The capital of Jordan is a modern city rich with ancient ruins.
- ❏ **Aqaba** - A port city on the Red Sea - popular for wind surfers and scuba divers as it is home to the Yamaniah coral reef in the Aqaba Marine Park.
- ❏ **Edom** - Ancient Biblical kingdom established by the Edomites.
- ❏ **Jabbok River** - The place where Jacob wrestled with God and was blessed by God.
- ❏ **Jerash Ruins** - Roman ruins going back 2000 years in time featuring the best preserved Roman provincial towns in the world.
- ❏ **Machaerus** - A hilltop fortress where John the Baptist was imprisoned and beheaded.
- ❏ **Madaba** - An ancient town in Jordan known for a 6th century mosaic map of the Holy Land in the Greek Orthodox Church of St. George.
- ❏ **Mount Nebo** - Moses stood on Mount Nebo before his death to view the Promised Land of Canaan after leading the children of Israel for 40 years.
- ❏ **Petra** - 'Rose City' archaeological fortress carved into the sandstone cliffs - also known as the lost city.

Holy Land Points of Interest

Jordan

- ❑ **Roman Theater** - Dating back to the period when the city was known as 'Philadelphia', this second century Roman theater with 6,000 seats is an archaeological and acoustical wonder.
- ❑ **The King's Highway** - The ancient Near East main trade route for centuries between Africa and Mesopotamia.
- ❑ **Umm Qais** - The ancient city of Gadara mentioned in the Bible as the site where Jesus cast out demons and sent them into the pigs which ran into the sea.
- ❑ **Wadi Mujib (Arnon River)** - A Biblical river canyon which enters the Dead Sea.
- ❑ **Wadi Rum** - This stunning desert features "moonscapes" of sandstone mountains and valleys and is home to several Bedouin tribes.

❑ _____

❑ _____

❑ _____

❑ _____

❑ _____

❑ _____

Holy Land Points of Interest

Egypt

- ☐ **Mara** - The desert springs by the Red Sea where the children of Israel found bitter water.
- ☐ **Mt. Sinai** - Rich in Biblical history of Moses and the children of Israel - from the burning bush, the Ten Commandments and the forging of the Golden Calf.
- ☐ **St. Catherine's Monastery** - The oldest working Christian monastery.
- ☐ **Synagogue of Ben Ezra** - The oldest Jewish synagogue in Egypt.
- ☐ **The 3 Pyramids of Giza** - One of the Seven Wonders of the World.
- ☐ **The Great Sphinx** - At the Pyramids of Chefren.

- ☐ _____

- ☐ _____

- ☐ _____

- ☐ _____

- ☐ _____

- ☐ _____

- ☐ _____

- ☐ _____

Holy Land Points of Interest

Greece

- ❑ **Athens** – Visit the Acropolis, Parthenon, Erectheum and Propylaea ruins.
- ❑ **Mars Hill** – Where the Apostle Paul preached regarding 'The Unknown God' as recorded in the Book of Acts in the New Testament.
- ❑ **Corinth** – Where Paul wrote his letters to the Corinthian Church.
- ❑ **Archaeological Museum** – This museum in Ancient Corinth houses many artifacts of local archaeological sites.
- ❑ **Ephesus** – The ancient Greek city where Paul spent two years of his ministry and was the church to whom he wrote his Ephesians epistle.
- ❑ **St. Johns Basilica** – Many believe this is where the apostle John was buried.
- ❑ **Temples of Diana** – One of the Seven Wonders of the ancient world.
- ❑ **Island of Patmos** – Where John wrote the Book of Revelation.

- ❑ _____

- ❑ _____

- ❑ _____

- ❑ _____

- ❑ _____

Holy Land Points of Interest

Unique Points of Interest and Adventures:

- ❑ 4x4 Jeep Tour to Places of Interest
- ❑ Abu Ghosh the Hummus Capital of the World
- ❑ Archaeological Digs
- ❑ Attend a 'Shuk' which is Arab for 'Outdoor Bazaar'
- ❑ Attend a Traditional Shabbat
- ❑ Beit Guvrin Caves
- ❑ Camel Ride
- ❑ Cherry Picking in Galilee
- ❑ Galilee Olive Oil Trail
- ❑ Get Baptized in the Jordan River
- ❑ Glass Bottom Boat Tour on the Red Sea
- ❑ Hot Air Balloon Ride
- ❑ Israeli Wine Tour
- ❑ Kosher Product Tasting
- ❑ Pool of Arches Ancient Water Reservoir
- ❑ Rosh HaNikra Grottoes
- ❑ Sample Street Food Like Falafel, Shawarma or Shakshooka
- ❑ Scuba Diving on the Red Sea
- ❑ Star Gazing in the Negev Desert at the Ramon Crater Nature Reserve
- ❑ Take Communion in Old City Jerusalem
- ❑ Tamar Festival at Masada
- ❑ The Jesus Trail
- ❑ The Nativity Trail
- ❑ White Water Rafting on the Northern Jordan River

Holy Land Points of Interest

Additional Sites to Visit:

❑ _____

❑ _____

❑ _____

❑ _____

❑ _____

❑ _____

❑ _____

❑ _____

❑ _____

❑ _____

❑ _____

❑ _____

❑ _____

❑ _____

❑ _____

Holy Land Points of Interest

Additional Sites to Visit:

❑ _____

❑ _____

❑ _____

❑ _____

❑ _____

❑ _____

❑ _____

❑ _____

❑ _____

❑ _____

❑ _____

❑ _____

❑ _____

❑ _____

❑ _____

1 *Holy Land Bucket List*

Site & Location: _____

_____

Why I Want To Visit Here: _____

_____

_____

My Holy Land Adventure Begins

Date Of Visit: _____

My Experience: _____

_____

_____

_____

_____

_____

What I Enjoyed Most: _____

_____

_____

The People I Met: _____

_____

_____

Holy Land Bucket List   **1**

_____

_____

_____

_____

_____

_____

_____

_____

_____

_____

_____

_____

_____

_____

_____

_____

_____

_____

_____

_____

_____

_____

_____

_____

_____

_____

_____

2 *Holy Land Bucket List*

Site & Location: _____

_____

Why I Want To Visit Here: _____

_____

_____

My Holy Land Adventure Begins

Date Of Visit: _____

My Experience: _____

_____

_____

_____

_____

_____

What I Enjoyed Most: _____

_____

_____

The People I Met: _____

_____

_____

Holy Land Bucket List   2

3 *Holy Land Bucket List*

Site & Location: _____

_____

Why I Want To Visit Here: _____

_____

_____

My Holy Land Adventure Begins

Date Of Visit: _____

My Experience: _____

_____

_____

_____

_____

What I Enjoyed Most: _____

_____

_____

The People I Met: _____

_____

_____

Holy Land Bucket List   3

4 *Holy Land Bucket List*

Site & Location: _____

_____

Why I Want To Visit Here: _____

_____

_____

My Holy Land Adventure Begins

Date Of Visit: _____

My Experience: _____

_____

_____

_____

_____

_____

What I Enjoyed Most: _____

_____

_____

The People I Met: _____

_____

_____

Holy Land Bucket List 4

_____

_____

_____

_____

_____

_____

_____

_____

_____

_____

_____

_____

_____

_____

_____

_____

_____

_____

_____

_____

_____

_____

_____

_____

5 *Holy Land Bucket List*

Site & Location: _____

_____

Why I Want To Visit Here: _____

_____

_____

My Holy Land Adventure Begins

Date Of Visit: _____

My Experience: _____

_____

_____

_____

_____

_____

What I Enjoyed Most: _____

_____

_____

The People I Met: _____

_____

_____

Holy Land Bucket List 5

6 Holy Land Bucket List

Site & Location: _____

_____

Why I Want To Visit Here: _____

_____

_____

My Holy Land Adventure Begins

Date Of Visit: _____

My Experience: _____

_____

_____

_____

_____

_____

What I Enjoyed Most: _____

_____

_____

The People I Met: _____

_____

_____

Holy Land Bucket List 6

7 *Holy Land Bucket List*

Site & Location: _____

_____

Why I Want To Visit Here: _____

_____

_____

My Holy Land Adventure Begins

Date Of Visit: _____

My Experience: _____

_____

_____

_____

_____

_____

What I Enjoyed Most: _____

_____

_____

The People I Met: _____

_____

_____

8 *Holy Land Bucket List*

Site & Location: _____

_____

Why I Want To Visit Here: _____

_____

_____

My Holy Land Adventure Begins

Date Of Visit: _____

My Experience: _____

_____

_____

_____

_____

_____

What I Enjoyed Most: _____

_____

_____

The People I Met: _____

_____

_____

Holy Land Bucket List 8

9 *Holy Land Bucket List*

Site & Location: _____

_____

Why I Want To Visit Here: _____

_____

_____

My Holy Land Adventure Begins

Date Of Visit: _____

My Experience: _____

_____

_____

_____

_____

_____

What I Enjoyed Most: _____

_____

_____

The People I Met: _____

_____

_____

Holy Land Bucket List 9

10 *Holy Land Bucket List*

Site & Location: _____

_____

Why I Want To Visit Here: _____

_____

_____

My Holy Land Adventure Begins

Date Of Visit: _____

My Experience: _____

_____

_____

_____

_____

_____

What I Enjoyed Most: _____

_____

_____

The People I Met: _____

_____

_____

Holy Land Bucket List 10

11 *Holy Land Bucket List*

Site & Location: _____

_____

Why I Want To Visit Here: _____

_____

_____

My Holy Land Adventure Begins

Date Of Visit: _____

My Experience: _____

_____

_____

_____

_____

_____

What I Enjoyed Most: _____

_____

_____

The People I Met: _____

_____

_____

Holy Land Bucket List 11

12 *Holy Land Bucket List*

Site & Location: _____

_____

Why I Want To Visit Here: _____

_____

_____

My Holy Land Adventure Begins

Date Of Visit: _____

My Experience: _____

_____

_____

_____

_____

_____

What I Enjoyed Most: _____

_____

_____

The People I Met: _____

_____

_____

_____
_____
_____
_____
_____
_____
_____
_____
_____
_____
_____
_____
_____
_____
_____
_____
_____
_____
_____
_____
_____
_____
_____
_____
_____
_____
_____
_____
_____

13 *Holy Land Bucket List*

Site & Location: _____

_____

Why I Want To Visit Here: _____

_____

_____

My Holy Land Adventure Begins

Date Of Visit: _____

My Experience: _____

_____

_____

_____

_____

_____

What I Enjoyed Most: _____

_____

_____

The People I Met: _____

_____

_____

14 *Holy Land Bucket List*

Site & Location: _____

_____

Why I Want To Visit Here: _____

_____

_____

My Holy Land Adventure Begins

Date Of Visit: _____

My Experience: _____

_____

_____

_____

_____

_____

What I Enjoyed Most: _____

_____

_____

The People I Met: _____

_____

_____

Holy Land Bucket List 14

_____

_____

_____

_____

_____

_____

_____

_____

_____

_____

_____

_____

_____

_____

_____

_____

_____

_____

_____

_____

_____

_____

_____

_____

_____

_____

15 *Holy Land Bucket List*

Site & Location: _____

_____

Why I Want To Visit Here: _____

_____

_____

My Holy Land Adventure Begins

Date Of Visit: _____

My Experience: _____

_____

_____

_____

_____

_____

What I Enjoyed Most: _____

_____

_____

The People I Met: _____

_____

_____

Holy Land Bucket List 15

16 *Holy Land Bucket List*

Site & Location: _____

_____

Why I Want To Visit Here: _____

_____

_____

My Holy Land Adventure Begins

Date Of Visit: _____

My Experience: _____

_____

_____

_____

_____

_____

What I Enjoyed Most: _____

_____

_____

The People I Met: _____

_____

_____

17 *Holy Land Bucket List*

Site & Location: _____

_____

Why I Want To Visit Here: _____

_____

_____

My Holy Land Adventure Begins

Date Of Visit: _____

My Experience: _____

_____

_____

_____

_____

_____

What I Enjoyed Most: _____

_____

_____

The People I Met: _____

_____

_____

Holy Land Bucket List 17

18 *Holy Land Bucket List*

Site & Location: _____

_____

Why I Want To Visit Here: _____

_____

_____

My Holy Land Adventure Begins

Date Of Visit: _____

My Experience: _____

_____

_____

_____

_____

_____

What I Enjoyed Most: _____

_____

_____

The People I Met: _____

_____

_____

Holy Land Bucket List 18

19 *Holy Land Bucket List*

Site & Location: _____

_____

Why I Want To Visit Here: _____

_____

_____

My Holy Land Adventure Begins

Date Of Visit: _____

My Experience: _____

_____

_____

_____

_____

_____

What I Enjoyed Most: _____

_____

_____

The People I Met: _____

_____

_____

Holy Land Bucket List 19

20 *Holy Land Bucket List*

Site & Location: _____

_____

Why I Want To Visit Here: _____

_____

_____

My Holy Land Adventure Begins

Date Of Visit: _____

My Experience: _____

_____

_____

_____

_____

_____

What I Enjoyed Most: _____

_____

_____

The People I Met: _____

_____

_____

Holy Land Bucket List 20

21 *Holy Land Bucket List*

Site & Location: _____

_____

Why I Want To Visit Here: _____

_____

_____

My Holy Land Adventure Begins

Date Of Visit: _____

My Experience: _____

_____

_____

_____

_____

_____

What I Enjoyed Most: _____

_____

_____

The People I Met: _____

_____

_____

22 *Holy Land Bucket List*

Site & Location: _____

_____

Why I Want To Visit Here: _____

_____

_____

My Holy Land Adventure Begins

Date Of Visit: _____

My Experience: _____

_____

_____

_____

_____

_____

What I Enjoyed Most: _____

_____

_____

The People I Met: _____

_____

_____

Holy Land Bucket List 22

23 *Holy Land Bucket List*

Site & Location: _____

_____

Why I Want To Visit Here: _____

_____

_____

My Holy Land Adventure Begins

Date Of Visit: _____

My Experience: _____

_____

_____

_____

_____

_____

What I Enjoyed Most: _____

_____

_____

The People I Met: _____

_____

_____

Holy Land Bucket List 23

---

24 *Holy Land Bucket List*

Site & Location: _____

_____

Why I Want To Visit Here: _____

_____

_____

My Holy Land Adventure Begins

Date Of Visit: _____

My Experience: _____

_____

_____

_____

_____

_____

What I Enjoyed Most: _____

_____

_____

The People I Met: _____

_____

_____

Holy Land Bucket List 24

25 *Holy Land Bucket List*

Site & Location: _____

_____

Why I Want To Visit Here: _____

_____

_____

My Holy Land Adventure Begins

Date Of Visit: _____

My Experience: _____

_____

_____

_____

_____

_____

What I Enjoyed Most: _____

_____

_____

The People I Met: _____

_____

_____

Holy Land Bucket List 25

26 *Holy Land Bucket List*

Site & Location: _____

_____

Why I Want To Visit Here: _____

_____

_____

My Holy Land Adventure Begins

Date Of Visit: _____

My Experience: _____

_____

_____

_____

_____

_____

What I Enjoyed Most: _____

_____

_____

_____

The People I Met: _____

_____

_____

27 *Holy Land Bucket List*

Site & Location: _____

_____

Why I Want To Visit Here: _____

_____

_____

My Holy Land Adventure Begins

Date Of Visit: _____

My Experience: _____

_____

_____

_____

_____

_____

What I Enjoyed Most: _____

_____

_____

The People I Met: _____

_____

_____

Holy Land Bucket List 27

28 Holy Land Bucket List

Site & Location: _____

_____

Why I Want To Visit Here: _____

_____

_____

My Holy Land Adventure Begins

Date Of Visit: _____

My Experience: _____

_____

_____

_____

_____

_____

What I Enjoyed Most: _____

_____

_____

The People I Met: _____

_____

_____

29 *Holy Land Bucket List*

Site & Location: _____

_____

Why I Want To Visit Here: _____

_____

_____

My Holy Land Adventure Begins

Date Of Visit: _____

My Experience: _____

_____

_____

_____

_____

_____

What I Enjoyed Most: _____

_____

_____

The People I Met: _____

_____

_____

30 *Holy Land Bucket List*

Site & Location: _____

_____

Why I Want To Visit Here: _____

_____

_____

My Holy Land Adventure Begins

Date Of Visit: _____

My Experience: _____

_____

_____

_____

_____

_____

What I Enjoyed Most: _____

_____

_____

The People I Met: _____

_____

_____

31 *Holy Land Bucket List*

Site & Location: _____

_____

Why I Want To Visit Here: _____

_____

_____

My Holy Land Adventure Begins

Date Of Visit: _____

My Experience: _____

_____

_____

_____

_____

_____

What I Enjoyed Most: _____

_____

_____

The People I Met: _____

_____

_____

Holy Land Bucket List 31

32 *Holy Land Bucket List*

Site & Location: _____

_____

Why I Want To Visit Here: _____

_____

_____

My Holy Land Adventure Begins

Date Of Visit: _____

My Experience: _____

_____

_____

_____

_____

_____

What I Enjoyed Most: _____

_____

_____

The People I Met: _____

_____

_____

33 *Holy Land Bucket List*

Site & Location: _____

_____

Why I Want To Visit Here: _____

_____

_____

My Holy Land Adventure Begins

Date Of Visit: _____

My Experience: _____

_____

_____

_____

_____

_____

What I Enjoyed Most: _____

_____

_____

The People I Met: _____

_____

_____

Holy Land Bucket List 33

34 *Holy Land Bucket List*

Site & Location: _____

_____

Why I Want To Visit Here: _____

_____

_____

My Holy Land Adventure Begins

Date Of Visit: _____

My Experience: _____

_____

_____

_____

_____

_____

What I Enjoyed Most: _____

_____

_____

The People I Met: _____

_____

_____

Holy Land Bucket List 34

35 *Holy Land Bucket List*

Site & Location: _____

_____

Why I Want To Visit Here: _____

_____

_____

My Holy Land Adventure Begins

Date Of Visit: _____

My Experience: _____

_____

_____

_____

_____

_____

What I Enjoyed Most: _____

_____

_____

The People I Met: _____

_____

_____

Holy Land Bucket List 35

36 *Holy Land Bucket List*

Site & Location: _____

_____

Why I Want To Visit Here: _____

_____

_____

My Holy Land Adventure Begins

Date Of Visit: _____

My Experience: _____

_____

_____

_____

_____

_____

What I Enjoyed Most: _____

_____

_____

The People I Met: _____

_____

_____

Holy Land Bucket List 36

37 *Holy Land Bucket List*

Site & Location: _____

_____

Why I Want To Visit Here: _____

_____

_____

My Holy Land Adventure Begins

Date Of Visit: _____

My Experience: _____

_____

_____

_____

_____

_____

What I Enjoyed Most: _____

_____

_____

The People I Met: _____

_____

_____

38 *Holy Land Bucket List*

Site & Location: _____

_____

Why I Want To Visit Here: _____

_____

_____

My Holy Land Adventure Begins

Date Of Visit: _____

My Experience: _____

_____

_____

_____

_____

_____

What I Enjoyed Most: _____

_____

_____

The People I Met: _____

_____

_____

Holy Land Bucket List 38

39 *Holy Land Bucket List*

Site & Location: _____

_____

Why I Want To Visit Here: _____

_____

_____

My Holy Land Adventure Begins

Date Of Visit: _____

My Experience: _____

_____

_____

_____

_____

_____

What I Enjoyed Most: _____

_____

_____

The People I Met: _____

_____

_____

Holy Land Bucket List 39

---

40 *Holy Land Bucket List*

Site & Location: _____

_____

Why I Want To Visit Here: _____

_____

_____

My Holy Land Adventure Begins

Date Of Visit: _____

My Experience: _____

_____

_____

_____

_____

_____

What I Enjoyed Most: _____

_____

_____

The People I Met: _____

_____

_____

_____

_____

_____

_____

_____

_____

_____

_____

_____

_____

_____

_____

_____

_____

_____

_____

_____

_____

_____

_____

_____

_____

_____

_____

_____

_____

_____

_____

_____

41 *Holy Land Bucket List*

Site & Location: _____

_____

Why I Want To Visit Here: _____

_____

_____

My Holy Land Adventure Begins

Date Of Visit: _____

My Experience: _____

_____

_____

_____

_____

_____

What I Enjoyed Most: _____

_____

_____

The People I Met: _____

_____

_____

42 *Holy Land Bucket List*

Site & Location: _____

_____

Why I Want To Visit Here: _____

_____

_____

My Holy Land Adventure Begins

Date Of Visit: _____

My Experience: _____

_____

_____

_____

_____

_____

What I Enjoyed Most: _____

_____

_____

The People I Met: _____

_____

_____

Holy Land Bucket List 42

_____

_____

_____

_____

_____

_____

_____

_____

_____

_____

_____

_____

_____

_____

_____

_____

_____

_____

_____

_____

_____

_____

_____

_____

_____

_____

_____

_____

_____

43 *Holy Land Bucket List*

Site & Location: _____

_____

Why I Want To Visit Here: _____

_____

_____

My Holy Land Adventure Begins

Date Of Visit: _____

My Experience: _____

_____

_____

_____

_____

_____

What I Enjoyed Most: _____

_____

_____

The People I Met: _____

_____

_____

44 *Holy Land Bucket List*

Site & Location: _____

_____

Why I Want To Visit Here: _____

_____

_____

My Holy Land Adventure Begins

Date Of Visit: _____

My Experience: _____

_____

_____

_____

_____

_____

What I Enjoyed Most: _____

_____

_____

The People I Met: _____

_____

_____

45 *Holy Land Bucket List*

Site & Location: _____

_____

Why I Want To Visit Here: _____

_____

_____

My Holy Land Adventure Begins

Date Of Visit: _____

My Experience: _____

_____

_____

_____

_____

_____

What I Enjoyed Most: _____

_____

_____

The People I Met: _____

_____

_____

46 *Holy Land Bucket List*

Site & Location: _____

_____

Why I Want To Visit Here: _____

_____

_____

My Holy Land Adventure Begins

Date Of Visit: _____

My Experience: _____

_____

_____

_____

_____

_____

What I Enjoyed Most: _____

_____

_____

The People I Met: _____

_____

_____

47 *Holy Land Bucket List*

Site & Location: _____

_____

Why I Want To Visit Here: _____

_____

_____

My Holy Land Adventure Begins

Date Of Visit: _____

My Experience: _____

_____

_____

_____

_____

_____

What I Enjoyed Most: _____

_____

_____

The People I Met: _____

_____

_____

48 Holy Land Bucket List

Site & Location: _____

_____

Why I Want To Visit Here: _____

_____

_____

My Holy Land Adventure Begins

Date Of Visit: _____

My Experience: _____

_____

_____

_____

_____

_____

What I Enjoyed Most: _____

_____

_____

The People I Met: _____

_____

_____

49 *Holy Land Bucket List*

Site & Location: _____

_____

Why I Want To Visit Here: _____

_____

_____

My Holy Land Adventure Begins

Date Of Visit: _____

My Experience: _____

_____

_____

_____

_____

_____

What I Enjoyed Most: _____

_____

_____

The People I Met: _____

_____

_____

50 *Holy Land Bucket List*

Site & Location: _____

_____

Why I Want To Visit Here: _____

_____

_____

My Holy Land Adventure Begins

Date Of Visit: _____

My Experience: _____

_____

_____

_____

_____

_____

What I Enjoyed Most: _____

_____

_____

The People I Met: _____

_____

_____

Holy Land Bucket List 50

Holy Land Adventure Highlights

Holy Land Adventure Highlights

Holy Land Adventure Highlights

Holy Land Adventure Highlights

Made in United States
North Haven, CT
21 September 2022

24299602R00076